Copyright © 2021 by
The Plastic Surgery Company

All rights reserved. No part of this book may be reproduced or used in any manner without written permission of the copyright owner except for the use of quotations in a book review. For more information, address: theplasticsurgerycompany@gmail.com.

First paperback edition, October 2021

Book design by Weiguang Ho

ISBN 979-8-4905-4087-8 (paperback)

Quick reference log

Date	Operation title	Page
		1-3
		4-6
		7-9
		10-12
		13-15
		16-18
		19-21
		22-24
		25-27
		28-30
		31-33
		34-36
		37-39
		40-42
		43-45
		46-48
		49-51
		52-54
		55-57
		58-60

Operation title

Date

Consultant

Anaesthetic

Equipment/instruments

Position

Indication

Incision

Findings

Procedure

Post-op plan

Illustration

Operation title

Date

Consultant

Anaesthetic

Equipment/instruments

Position

Indication

Incision

Findings

Procedure

Post-op plan

Illustration

Operation title

Date

Consultant

Anaesthetic

Equipment/instruments

Position

Indication

Incision

Findings

Procedure

Post-op plan

Illustration

Operation title

Date

Consultant

Anaesthetic

Equipment/instruments

Position

Indication

Incision

Findings

Procedure

Post-op plan

Illustration

Operation title

Date

Consultant

Anaesthetic

Equipment/instruments

Position

Indication

Incision

Findings

Procedure

Post-op plan

Illustration

Operation title

Date

Consultant

Anaesthetic

Equipment/instruments

Position

Indication

Incision

Findings

Procedure

Post-op plan

Illustration

Operation title

Date

Consultant

Anaesthetic

Equipment/instruments

Position

Indication

Incision

Findings

Procedure

Post-op plan

Illustration

Operation title

Date

Consultant

Anaesthetic

Equipment/instruments

Position

Indication

Incision

Findings

Procedure

Post-op plan

Illustration

Operation title

Date

Consultant

Anaesthetic

Equipment/instruments

Position

Indication

Incision

Findings

Procedure

Post-op plan

Illustration

Operation title

Date

Consultant

Anaesthetic

Equipment/instruments

Position

Indication

Incision

Findings

Procedure

Post-op plan

Illustration

Operation title

Date

Consultant

Anaesthetic

Equipment/instruments

Position

Indication

Incision

Findings

Procedure

Post-op plan

Illustration

Operation title

Date

Consultant

Anaesthetic

Equipment/instruments

Position

Indication

Incision

Findings

Procedure

Post-op plan

Illustration

Operation title

Date

Consultant

Anaesthetic

Equipment/instruments

Position

Indication

Incision

Findings

Procedure

Post-op plan

Illustration

Operation title

Date

Consultant

Anaesthetic

Equipment/instruments

Position

Indication

Incision

Findings

Procedure

Post-op plan

Illustration

Operation title

Date

Consultant

Anaesthetic

Equipment/instruments

Position

Indication

Incision

Findings

Procedure

Post-op plan

Illustration

Operation title

Date

Consultant

Anaesthetic

Equipment/instruments

Position

Indication

Incision

Findings

Procedure

Post-op plan

Illustration

Operation title

Date

Consultant

Anaesthetic

Equipment/instruments

Position

Indication

Incision

Findings

Procedure

Post-op plan

Illustration

Operation title

Date

Consultant

Anaesthetic

Equipment/instruments

Position

Indication

Incision

Findings

Procedure

Post-op plan

Illustration

Operation title

Date

Consultant

Anaesthetic

Equipment/instruments

Position

Indication

Incision

Findings

Procedure

Post-op plan

Illustration

Operation title

Date

Consultant

Anaesthetic

Equipment/instruments

Position

Indication

Incision

Findings

Procedure

Post-op plan

Illustration

Printed in Great Britain
by Amazon